GIBRALTAR

Photographs: J. Marc Linares, Xavier Durán, Creativa Fotos Aéreas and FISA-Escudo de Oro, S. A. Photographic Archives.

Literary text, design, lay-out and printing completely created by the technical department of EDITORIAL ESCUDO DE ORO S.A.

Palaudàries, 26 - 08004 Barcelona (Spain).

www.eoro.com
e-mail: editorial@eoro.com

Editorial Escudo de Oro, S.A.

Aerial view of the Rock of Gibraltar, La Línea de la Concepción (Spain), the bay and the African coast.

GEOGRAPHY AND CLIMATE

Gibraltar, a British enclave with an extension of barely 6 km^2, with part of its land gained from the sea, is located in the most southern extremity of the Iberian peninsula, next to the Bay of Algeciras with a dominating position over the narrow strait that bears its name. This strategic position between the Mediterranean Sea and the Atlantic Ocean, between Europe and Africa, and its famous Rock are, undoubtedly, the two geographical aspects that most influenced its history.

In ancient times, this imposing lime rock that reaches up to 419 metres in altitude, was an island that later was joined to the peninsula by a sand isthmus. At present this isthmus, where the border with Spain is located, is somewhat wider thanks to the enlargement of its airport during the Second World War. The Winston Churchill Avenue, which passes through the airport runway, is the access road to the city of Gibraltar that extends on a two-kilometre strip between the Rock and the bay, with land partially gained from the sea. On the western side you find the port of Gibraltar.

On the eastern or levantine side, the Rock has a more jagged and steep aspect. On this side, there is room only for abrupt cliffs, three beaches considered the best ones of the enclave, and a skilful work of engineering for the storage of rainwater, with a base made of metallic sheets fixed in the rock.

On the southern extreme of the Rock there is the Punta Europa, with its lighthouse, at a distance of only 14 kilometres from the African coast.

Now we still have to describe the Rock itself, which hides a great many galleries and caves in its interior, some of them are natural and others were dug out during war times. Legend even mentions one that communicates with Africa under the Strait.

It has a pleasantly mild Mediterranean climate, and it very seldom rains between May and October. In winter the average temperature is of 15°C and in summer, of 23°C. The variations depend especially on the winds. The most characteristic are the west wind, which is very dry, and the east wind, more humid. In winter, occasional cold winds from the North bring the temperature down to 6° C.

Aerial view of the West side of the Rock.

Aerial view of the East side of the Rock. *Aerial view of the South side of the Rock.* 

A BRIEF HISTORICAL OUTLINE

A cranium from the Neanderthal period (around 50,000 BC) which was found in one of the caves of the Rock in 1848, now exhibited in the Gibraltar Museum, represents the most ancient imprint of human presence in this enclave. The following references bring us 4,000 years back: with its imposing outline, Mount Calpe as the Greeks named it, signalled the limit to the first navigators coming from the East. Daring to cross the strong currents of the Strait with their rudimentary boats could make it difficult and even impossible for them to return. Calpe Mount was one of the pillars of Melkart, the Tyrian solar God, called Heracles by the Greeks and Hercules by the Romans, with the Abila Mount, on the other side of the Strait, near Ceuta, indicating the entrance of the home of this god in the Atlantic.
In the year 711 the area was occupied by the troops of Tarik Ben Zayed, the Arab leader who conquered the peninsula, and established a fortress called Gibel Tarik («mountain of Tarik»), the name of Gibraltar coming from there. However, the remains of Muslim

Monument next to the Spanish border reflecting the main historical events of Gibraltar.

constructions that have been preserved until now are from a later period following Tarik, starting from 1160, the year when Abdul Memen, caliph of Morocco, founded the city on the Rock, with its fortress, its walls, its mosques, its water channels, etc. The new city was designed as a strong fortress to protect the transport of everything necessary from Africa in case the Muslim army was obligated to start fighting against the Christians.

In 1309 Gibraltar was captured by the Spanish troops of Fernando IV lead by Guzmán El Bueno. But in 1333 the city fell back into Muslim hands. The Tower of the Moorish Castle was built then, and the streets in the lower part of the city were urbanised. In 1462, after several attempts, the Duke of Medina Sidonia finally conquered Gibraltar, and in 1502, because of its strategic military significance, the Catholic Kings incorporated it to the Kingdom of Castille. In 1502, Queen Isabel gave the coat of arms, the castle and the key to the city.

After the start of the Spanish Succession War, and in the name of Archduke Carlos, on the 2nd of August 1704, the Anglo-Dutch army under the command of admiral Rocke captured Gibraltar.

And although the French candidate finally won, and was proclaimed King of Spain with the name of Felipe V, the cession of Gibraltar and of the island of Minorca to Great Britain by the Utrecht Treaty (1713) was recognised.

Later attempts on the part of Spain to reclaim the fort were in vain. In 1726 the first siege took place, and between 1779 and 1783, the so-called Great Siege. With the North American Independence War (1878), Spain, an ally of France, offered its neutrality to Great Britain in exchange for the cession of Gibraltar, which Great Britain refused. The Great Siege started on the 21st of June 1779, and Spanish forces then had up to 33,000 soldiers at their disposal facing a garrison of 7,000 men that had taken refuge on the Rock. The siege lasted more than three years during which the Rock remained cut off, and the garrison was saved from starvation thanks to three reliefs of the Royal Navy: the first, in January 1780, the second, April 1781 and the third October 1782.

Monument to the Columns of Hercules, on the Southern side of the Rock.

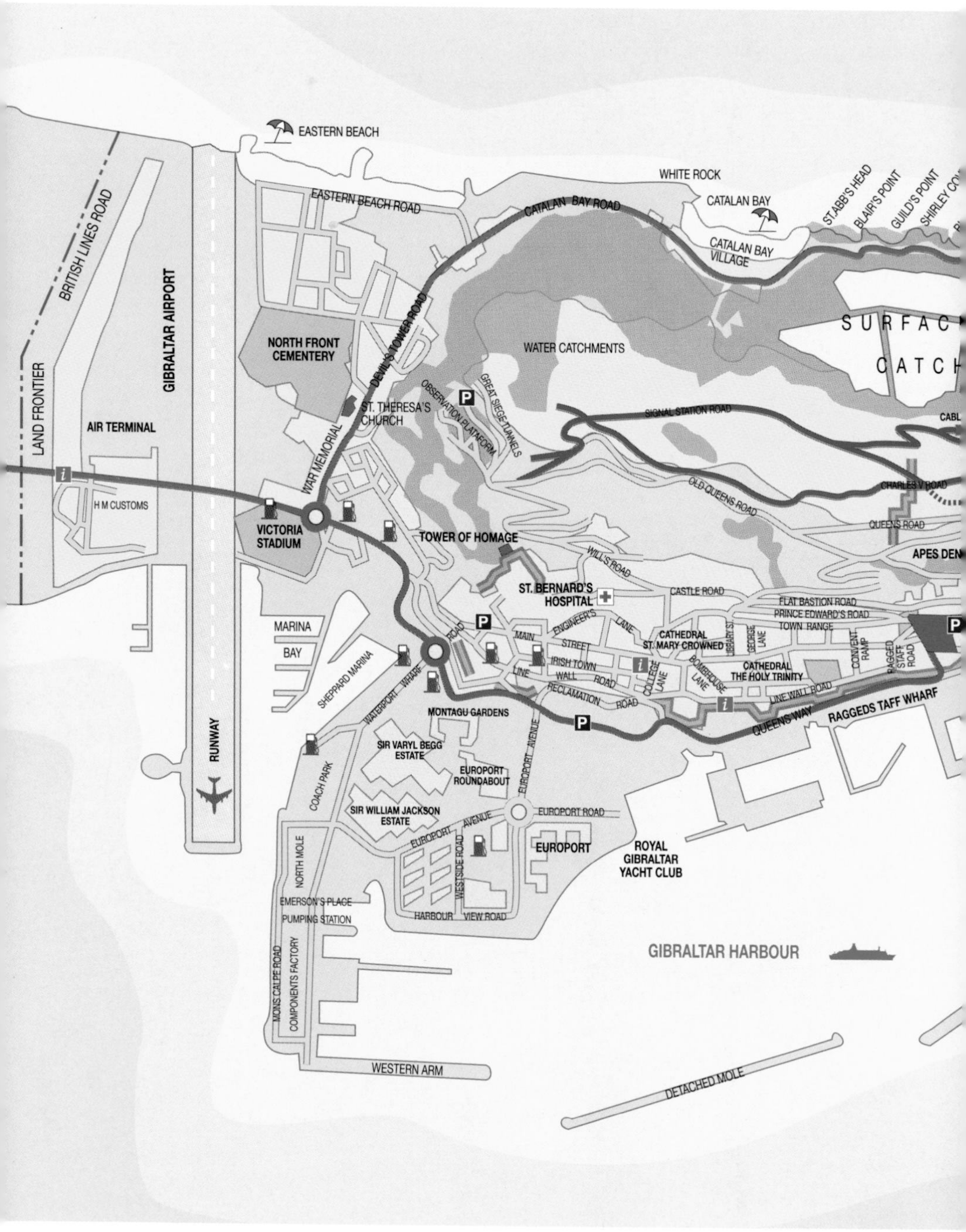

EASTERN BEACH
WHITE ROCK
CATALAN BAY
ST.ABB'S HEAD
BLAIR'S POINT
GUILD'S POINT
EASTERN BEACH ROAD
CATALAN BAY ROAD
CATALAN BAY VILLAGE
BRITISH LINES ROAD
GIBRALTAR AIRPORT
LAND FRONTIER
NORTH FRONT CEMENTERY
DEVIL'S TOWER ROAD
WATER CATCHMENTS
SURFAC
CATCH
AIR TERMINAL
ST. THERESA'S CHURCH
OBSERVATION PLATAFORM
GREAT SIEGE TUNNELS
SIGNAL STATION ROAD
WAR MEMORIAL
H M CUSTOMS
OLD QUEENS ROAD
CHARLES V ROAD
QUEENS ROAD
VICTORIA STADIUM
TOWER OF HOMAGE
WILL'S ROAD
APES DEN
ST. BERNARD'S HOSPITAL
CASTLE ROAD
FLAT BASTION ROAD
PRINCE EDWARD'S ROAD
TOWN RANGE
MARINA BAY
ROAD
MAIN STREET
ENGINEER'S LANE
CATHEDRAL ST. MARY CROWNED
LIBRARY ST.
GEORGE LANE
CONVENT RAMP
RAGGED STAFF ROAD
IRISH TOWN
LINE WALL ROAD
COLLEGE LANE
BOMBHOUSE LANE
CATHEDRAL THE HOLY TRINITY
SHEPPARD MARINA
WATERPORT WHARF
RECLAMATION ROAD
LINE WALL ROAD
QUEENS WAY
RAGGEDS TAFF WHARF
MONTAGU GARDENS
SIR VARYL BEGG ESTATE
EUROPORT ROUNDABOUT
EUROPORT AVENUE
RUNWAY
COACH PARK
SIR WILLIAM JACKSON ESTATE
EUROPORT ROAD
EUROPORT AVENUE
WESTSIDE ROAD
EUROPORT
ROYAL GIBRALTAR YACHT CLUB
NORTH MOLE
EMERSON'S PLACE
PUMPING STATION
HARBOUR VIEW ROAD
GIBRALTAR HARBOUR
MONS CALPE ROAD
COMPONENTS FACTORY
WESTERN ARM
DETACHED MOLE

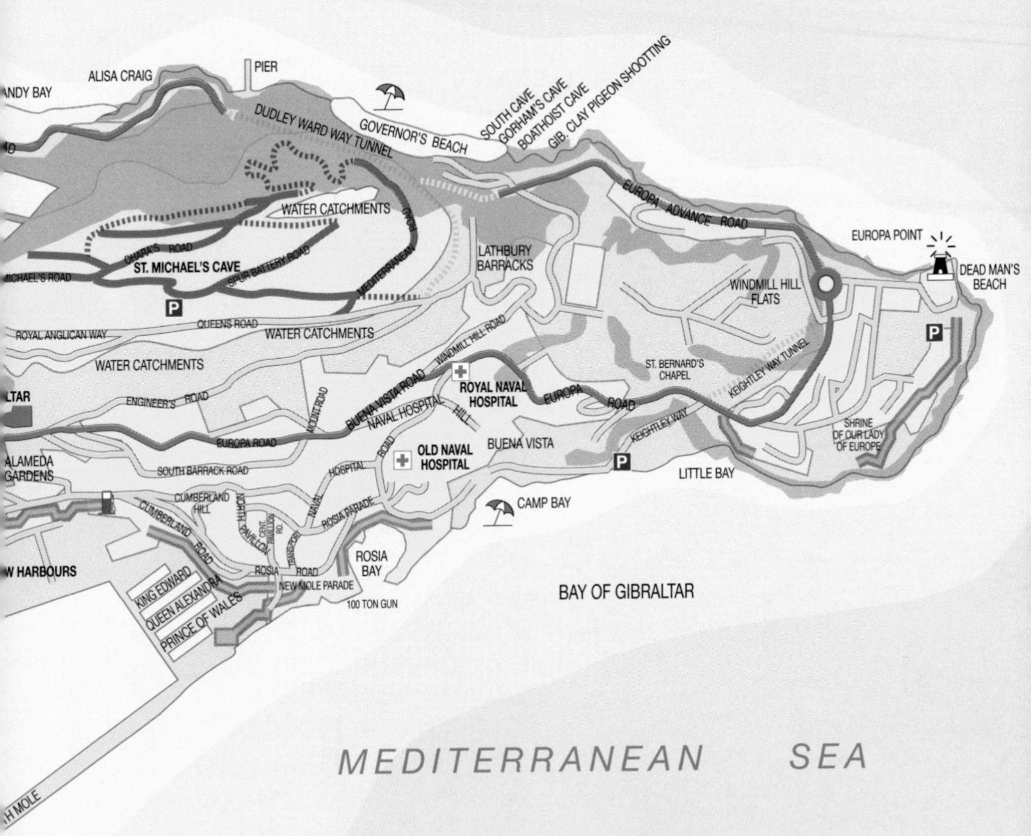
ALISA CRAIG
PIER
DUDLEY WARD WAY TUNNEL
GOVERNOR'S BEACH
SOUTH CAVE
GORHAM'S CAVE
BOATHOIST CAVE
GIB. CLAY PIGEON SHOOTING
WATER CATCHMENTS
O'HARA'S ROAD
ST. MICHAEL'S CAVE
SPUR BATTERY ROAD
MEDITERRANEAN ROAD
LATHBURY BARRACKS
EUROPA ADVANCE ROAD
EUROPA POINT
DEAD MAN'S BEACH
WINDMILL HILL FLATS
QUEENS ROAD
ROYAL ANGLICAN WAY
WATER CATCHMENTS
WATER CATCHMENTS
WINDMILL HILL ROAD
ST. BERNARD'S CHAPEL
KEIGHTLEY WAY TUNNEL
ENGINEER'S ROAD
BUENA VISTA ROAD
ROYAL NAVAL HOSPITAL
EUROPA ROAD
NAVAL HOSPITAL HILL
MOUNT ROAD
EUROPA ROAD
OLD NAVAL HOSPITAL
BUENA VISTA
KEIGHTLEY WAY
SHRINE OF OUR LADY OF EUROPE
ALAMEDA GARDENS
SOUTH BARRACK ROAD
HOSPITAL ROAD
LITTLE BAY
CUMBERLAND HILL
CUMBERLAND ROAD
NORTH PAVILLON
CENT. PAVILLON RD.
NAVAL
TRANSPORT
ROSIA PARADE
CAMP BAY
ROSIA BAY
ROSIA ROAD
NEW MOLE PARADE
100 TON GUN
KING EDWARD
QUEEN ALEXANDRA
PRINCE OF WALES
BAY OF GIBRALTAR
MEDITERRANEAN SEA

N
NE
E
SE
S
SW
W
NW

Night view of the Rock.

Finally, the United States gained their independence and peace was established. The siege ended on the 2nd of February 1783. With the Treaty of Versailles Minorca was given back to Spain and Great Britain was confirmed in its possession of Gibraltar. The reconstruction of the city, which was completely destroyed by the large siege, started. Later on, in 1830, Gibraltar was declared a colony. After the Great Siege there were no new military attempts on the part of Spain to try to reclaim the Rock, although recently, a different type of siege took place when the border was closed between 1969 and 1985 with the subsequent economic blockade.

In 1704, following the English conquest of Gibraltar, the majority of its Spanish inhabitants moved to the new San Roque nucleus and those who stayed, left it during the siege of 1726. Immigrants started coming, especially from Genoa, Portugal and also Moroccan Jews who, together with a handful of Englishmen who had settled there, made up a new community of inhabitants. Later on, when Great Britain and Spain became allies in the wars against Napoleon, a considerable number of Spaniards, as well as a group of English citizens from Malta, came to live in Gibraltar. At present, the population of Gibraltar is of 30.000 inhabitants, and although the majority are catholic and also speak Spanish, Anglicans, Protestants, Jews, Muslims and Hindus live together.

The XIXth century was a very prosperous period for Gibraltar: During the war against Napoleon it became an important commercial centre for the Royal Navy battle cruisers and for the English corsairs taking the boats they captured from the enemy to sell them as loot. And as a result of the opening of the Suez Canal (1869), it acquired a considerable strategic importance as a mandatory pass for commerce between Great Britain and India.

During the First World War, Gibraltar served as a support base for the supplies to British troops, although it could not impede the passage of German submarines towards the Mediterranean. Its military strategic significance was confirmed during the Second World War as the bridgehead for the allies in the Mediterranean. For that very reason, the North American squad that later on dis-

The Rock seen from La Línea de la Concepción in Spain.

The Sun Dial, in the city entrance.

The Rock from Algeciras. ▷

embarked in North Africa, gathered in its port.

To a great measure, its economy has been traditionally connected with its role as a naval base, but also as a free port converting it into an important commercial centre since the beginning of the XVIIIth century.

With regard to its government, as a colony of the British Crown, Gibraltar is under the jurisdiction of the Foreign Office and of the Commonwealth. The Parliament of Gibraltar has its headquarters in the House of Assembly, located on Main Street, and is made up of 18 deputies, 15 of them elected by popular vote, whereas the Secretary of Finances and the Public Prosecutor of the Crown are functionaries, and the Speaker or Chamber President is elected by the rest of deputies. The Governor, a high rank official from the armed forces, is appointed by the British government and has the supreme responsibility of the government and welfare of the enclave. His residence is also on Main Street, in a complex known as The Convent.

With regard to laws, they are very similar to the British laws, and the educational scheme follows the British standard.

EL CHISPA
LA LINEA
GL·3·400

A Monkey from Gibraltar on the observation post of the Rock.

FAUNA AND FLORA

The famous monkeys are undoubtedly one of the most renowned aspects of Gibraltar. Their main characteristic is that they have no tail and belong to the Macaca Sylvanus species which, in the wild, can only be found in Morocco, Algeria and Gibraltar. Their origin on the Rock is unknown, as there are no written references of their presence until the XVIIIth century. Legend tells that they emigrated from Morocco through a tunnel under the Strait. More scientific theories tell that they probably came with the first Arab invaders, or that they were brought towards the beginning of the British rule to provide entertainment to this remote boring post of the Empire. Another legend says that the day they disappear, Gibraltar will cease to be British. At present, there are more than a hundred of them: their birth and death are registered and they all have a name. They are under the control and responsibility of the government of Gibraltar, since the beginning of the XXth century and the army takes care of their food and peaceful coexistence. There are two colonies of monkeys: a group

A great number of dolphins live in the waters of the bay.

of 20 resides in Apes' Den, next to Queen's Gate, and the rest of them, in the area of the Great Siege, are more difficult to see. The monkeys from the first group often come close to the tourists and beg for something to eat or even try to steal anything they can from them. They seldom go near the high part of the city.

The slopes of the Rock are also the home of other animals such as rabbits, porcupines and rattlesnakes. Tourists will enjoy observing the great number of dolphins that live in the bay, where they find food and breed in the summer. Several agencies organise dolphin safaris so you can have a close look at those cetaceans.

The bay and the turbulent waters of the Strait give shelter to many other marine species. The most characteristic fish of the gastronomy of Gibraltar surely is the swordfish but you can also eat sole, red mullet, red bream, seabass, mackerel, etc. For the ornithologists, the southern peak of the Rock is a mythical point, because in the spring and fall hundreds of migratory birds cross over the Strait. Some of those species use the whirlwind as the necessary momentum on their way to the tropical areas of Africa. With regard to

A seagull resting on one of the cannons of the Rock.

the birds that live in Gibraltar we can mention the Moorish partridge, the common sparrow, the blackbird, the hoopoe, the blackcap warbler, the reed warbler, the wren and the peregrine falcon.
In the top part, the flora of the Rock comprises pine trees, eucalyptus and wild olive trees, most of them were planted in the XIXth century to prevent land erosion. In the lower part there is a great variety of bushes and plants such as the broom, jacarandas, palm, bougainvillaea, honeysuckle, lavender and jasmine.

The Rock and the Alameda.

Casemates Gates with the Moorish Castle in the background.

THE CITY OF GIBRALTAR

The old quarters of Gibraltar extend along a narrow fringe between the Rock and the port. Main Street, also called Royal Street, crosses from north to south and is its main artery. Remains of the old walls and other defences show evidence of the old city borders. On the northern side of Main Street where the **Casemates Gate** stands, which was completely rebuilt after the Great Siege, and on the southern side of Main street, the **Southport Gate**. The latter has three gates: the oldest dates from the XVIth century and displays the Spanish coat of arms flanked with the two columns of Hercules and at the bottom, the Gibraltar coat of arms and the Golden Fleece. The second gate, matching the first one, displays the coats of arms of the British, of Gibraltar and of Sir John Adye, a general who was governor in 1883, the year it was inaugurated. And the third gate called **New Gate**, was opened in 1967 to improve the influx of traffic.
In the east, the Rock and the Moorish Castle protected the city and in the west the **Line**

Southport Gate.

New Gate.

American War Memorial.

Main street or Royal street. ▷

Wall also called the sea wall, because the sea formerly reached the foot of this wall. The Line Wall is part of the defensive system that goes all the way to Punta Europa on the southern side. Initially, it was built by the Muslims and was reinforced throughout its history. More recently its level was lowered and deep terraces were added for the artillery. In the section that corresponds to the old city, the **American War Memorial** was erected in 1932 to celebrate the great achievements and the friendship between the United States forces and Great Britain during the First World War.

Main street is a busy street, especially along the first section where you can get anything you want in its great many shops. On the right-hand side, going towards the sea, you find the **Irish Town**, with its many pubs, where you can breathe the purest English atmosphere. On Main street and along the surrounding streets, many houses still preserve the colonial flavour on their facades, some of them with beautiful forged iron balconies. Going along Main street towards the south, on John Mackintosh

Sapphire
The Horseshoe Bar - Café

Perspective of the "Piazza" with the City Hall.

Square, better known as the **Piazza**, the **House of Assembly** and the **City Hall** stand. Both are from the beginning of the XIXth century, formerly the Commercial Library and the home of a wealthy local merchant.
Further along Main Street you will find the **Cathedral of St. Mary the Crowned**, of Catholic cult. It stands in the place of the old mosque of Gibraltar, and was consecrated as a Christian parish by the Spanish following their conquest of the Rock. It was seriously damaged during the Great Siege and was completely reconstructed.

On the nearby Bomb House Lane you will find the **Great Synagogue**, the most important of the four synagogues on the Rock, a building from 1801 with its main entrance on Line Wall Road, and the **Museum of Gibraltar**. All the history of this enclave is gathered in the museum. It exhibits an extraordinary piece, the so-called cranium of Gibraltar, found in 1848 in one of the caves of the Rock, the first Neanderthal specimen found in Europe. In the basement the museum preserves the remains of the Arab baths from the XIVth century. Two rooms are especially dedicated to the 1704 British invasion and to the Great Siege, and a big scale model reproduces all the streets of the city, so you can get to know Gibraltar as it was in 1865, when the port was still to be built and the land had not yet been gained from the sea. A section of the museum is also dedicated to natural life on the Rock.

Very near the Museum of Gibraltar, the Anglican **Cathedral of the Holy Trinity**, is a building with obvious Arab reminiscences. Its construction started in 1825 and in 1838 it was consecrated as a cathedral, in a ceremony presided by Queen Adelaide, widow of William IV.

Going back to Main street, down Library street you get directly to **Governor's Parade**. There are two interesting buildings on this square: **St. Andrew Church of Scotland**, from 1854, and the **Garrison Library**, from 1804. In addition to being an important library, it also is the residence of the local newspaper, the "Gibraltar Chronicle", founded in 1801, the first newspaper to publish Nelson's victory in the battle of Trafalgar (October 21st 1805).

On the last section of Main street

Cathedral of St Mary the Crowned.

Cathedral of the Holy Trinity: interior and exterior.

The cannons of the Governor's House.

you will find the complex of **The Convent**, which since 1704 is the residence of the governor of Gibraltar. From the original Franciscan convent built in the XVIth there is still the magnificent cloister, but this part of the building cannot be visited. The facade was reconstructed in the XIXth century in gothic style with red bricks. You can visit **King's Chapel**, originally Saint Francis' Chapel, which was converted into an Anglican Church for the garrison after the British occupation. Every Tuesday, at eleven, the change of the guards takes place in front of the Convent, although for reasons of security, on many occasions this ceremony does not take place.
And finally, right before you get to the Southport Gate, you will find the **John Mackintosh Hall**, the cultural centre with its pleasant indoor patio. It was inaugurated in 1964 and was created by John Mackintosh to promote English culture and to strengthen its bonds with Great Britain. Next to the Southport Gates you will find the **Cemetery of Trafalgar**, where some of the men who died during this battle are buried as well as the garrison's officials and their relatives.

Two aspects of the change of the guards in front of the main facade of The Convent or Governor's House.

Graves from the Cemetery of Gibraltar.

SCHOOL
CHILDREN
CROSSING

The Tower of Homage of the Moorish Castle.

The Tower of Homage and the bay. ▷

THE MOORISH CASTLE

North of the Rock, in a privileged place overlooking both the city and the bay, stands the Tower of Homage, the section of the old Moorish Castle that is best preserved. Next to the tower there are also some parts of the walls and small towers belonging to the castle, although the whole area is so urbanised that it is difficult to get an idea of its old layout. Built in the XIIth century when the city was founded by Abdul Memen, caliph of Morocco, and reinforced towards the middle of the XIVth century, period that corresponds to the Tower of Homage, the Moorish Castle constituted a large fortified complex with three different enclosures. In the highest part, the Tower of Homage, under which the Qasbah lay, was the entrance to the castle. Lower down, and separated by a wall, there was the so called "Old Town", with the Earth Gate, and then, also separated by a wall, the area called La Barcina, with the shipyard and the Sea Gate, subsequently replaced by the actual Gates of Casemates, once bordering the sea.

Staging with full size figures in the Tunnels of the Great Siege.

THE EXHIBITION "GIBRALTAR, A CITY UNDER SIEGE" AND THE TUNNELS OF THE GREAT SIEGE

Further up from the Moorish Castle and the Tower of Homage there is a building known as **Willis' Magazine**. It is one of the first constructions the British built for the storage of ammunitions when they occupied the Rock in 1704,. However, this functional building hides an interesting feature: the signatures and graffiti left on the walls by soldiers keeping watch, the oldest of them dating back to 1726, most probably to keep busy during those long hours and maybe to fight sleeping, which in those days was punished with death. At present, it hosts the **Exhibition "Gibraltar, a City Under Siege"**, dedicated to the famous episode of the Rock and an excellent antechamber before going to the Tunnels of the Great Siege.
The road up to the tunnels first goes through **The Military Heritage Centre**, set up in one of the many batteries built in the Rock. This particular one, called the battery of Princess Caroline, was built in 1732, and compris-

es several rooms that still preserve the hoist to load the artillery and other devices from that period. In one of the rooms you can see a list of the Regiments that served Gibraltar since 1704.

The Tunnels of the Great Siege started on May 25th 1782 with the so-called Windsor Gallery. Sergeant Major Ince had the idea of digging a tunnel all the way to the area called Notch, an inaccessible natural platform on the north side of the Rock, to install cannons there to aim at the Spanish positions on the isthmus, an idea governor Elliot approved of and encouraged. Armed with sledgehammers, perforated crowbars, and with explosives, 18 men excavated a tunnel 25 metres long in five weeks. After the Great Siege construction went on, with rooms like St. George Hall, with seven loopholes for cannons, and the Cornwallis Room. The building of the network of tunnels continued during later periods and especially during the Second World War. Throughout the Rock, there is an approximate total extension of more than 50 km in

Three important characters of the Tunnels of the Great Siege: Sergeant Major Ince, the architect of the tunnels, governor Elliot and captain Curtis.

length, the majority of them on military grounds.
The part that can be visited is about 200 metres long, with an average height of 2.10 metres and 1.83 width. They are set with full size figures representing several moments of the Great Siege, and the digging of the tunnels. In the entrance and in the galleries you can admire several cannons from Victorian times and one from the XVIIIth century. The visit ends on the observation point overlooking the Mediterranean on the northern side.

Representations of the digging works of during the Great Siege and the Second World War.

Auditorium of Saint Michael's Cave.

SAINT MICHAEL'S CAVE

Of the 140 caves the Rock hides, it is the only one opened to the public, and according to the legend it connects with Africa through a secret passageway under the waters of the Strait. St. Michael's Cave, spectacular for its stalactites and stalagmites formations, was already known in prehistoric times. It has a big cave on the top part that connects with a smaller one through five passageways between 12.2 and 45.7 metres.

Other smaller passageways lead to smaller caves, the deepest one is 62.5 metres below the entrance level.

The big cave is now an auditorium where concerts, dance shows and theatre performances are celebrated. During the Second World War the cave was converted into an emergency hospital, although, its use was not necessary during the war.

During the works of demolition to open another entrance to the cave, a lower level with more caves was discovered, and a small lake.

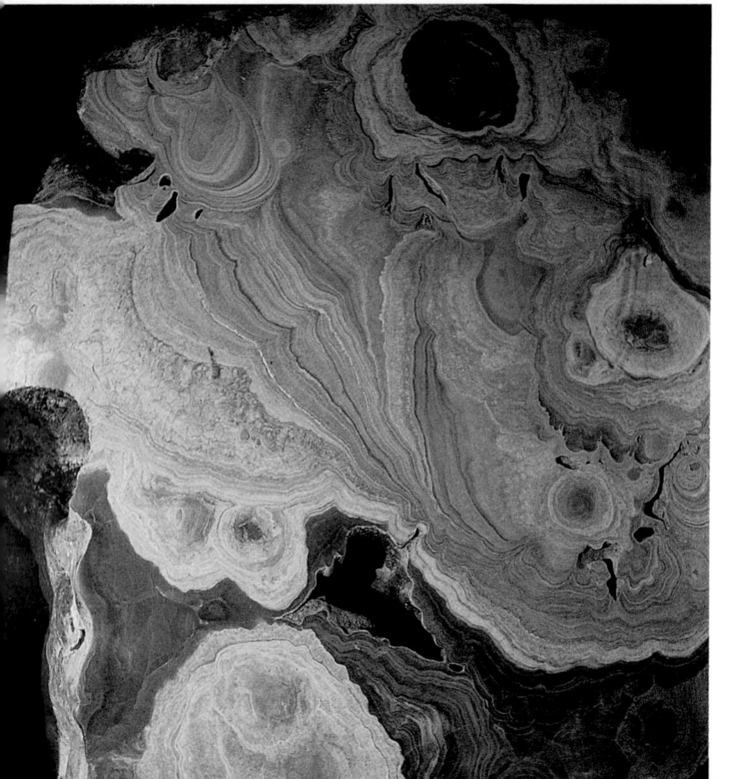

Two aspects of the gigantic stalactites and stalagmites of Saint Michael's Cave.

A 45-cm section cut from a stalactite in 1972. The rings represent the sediments deposited by the water through time. The darkest areas indicate periods of lesser rain, while the two white lines are thought to correspond with ice periods.

EXIT

View of the Port of Gibraltar from the Rock.

THE PORT

The port of Gibraltar and the Marina Bay, are both situated on the western side, and were built almost entirely on land gained from the sea. After the Spanish conquest, a breakwater was built which, between the XVIIIth and XIXth century, was replaced by a port designed as the Mediterranean base for the Royal Navy. During the battle of Trafalgar it was Admiral Nelson's main base. The way we know it today is thanks to the enlargement realised towards the end of the Victorian reign, a period when the Royal Navy with its battleships was the queen of the seas. Its strategic value was made clear during the two world wars, to control the entrance and exit of boats towards the Mediterranean, and also as a base for the allied fleet that disembarked in North Africa in 1942. At present, the Royal Navy only occupies a small part of the port and the docks are used for the repair and maintenance of merchant ships.

Two aspects of Marina Bay.

The cable car and the port.

The Rock from the restaurant observation point at the end of the cable car itinerary.

THE SOUTH OF GIBRALTAR AND PUNTA EUROPA

Next to the Southport Gate there is an area known as "South District", offering several interesting features. When you cross the gate, you reach **the Cable Car Station**. This excursion to the top of the Rock will allow you to enjoy wonderful panoramic views of Gibraltar, of the Mediterranean, of the Strait and even of Africa on a good clear day. In all, the Cable Car covers a distance of 673 metres and between the first and the last stop, it goes up 352 metres in height. The middle stop drops you very near **Apes' Den**, next to Queen's Gate. At the last stop there is a cafeteria-restaurant service.

The highest point of the Rock (419 m) is further south, next to the **O'Hara Battery**, and you can drive up there or walk up the Mediterranean Steps. In the O'Hara Battery you can also admire two spectacular cannons. They have a 233-mm opening and could send projectiles of almost 250 kilos. During the

Observation post and monument of the Columns of Hercules. In the background you can make out the African coast.

Second World War, from this strategic position at an altitude of more than 400 metres, the most powerful weapons defended the waters of the Strait. Other observation posts in the southern part on top of the Rock are the **Spur Battery** and next to the monument to the Columns of Hercules.
Sir George Don, the governor of Gibraltar, inaugurated the gar-

Detail of the Alameda Gardens.

dens of La Alameda, next to the lower cable car station, in 1816, to provide this military enclave with a pleasant place for walking. It was financed by means of voluntary contributions and with the profits from the public lottery organised by the governor himself. In 1991 it became the Botanical Garden, an outdoor theatre with a capacity for 435 guests, a monument to Governor Elliot and another dedicated to the Duke of Wellington.

Right on top of the gardens you can see **The Rock Hotel**, one of the most classical and luxurious hotels of Gibraltar and the **Casino**.

Further south, following the port, you have the Rosia Bay and **Camp Bay,** the only beach west of Gibraltar. **Rosia Bay** was created as a base for the Royal Navy towards the end of the XVIIIth century, during the Napoleonic wars. And it is also the place where the Victory anchored, carrying the lifeless body of admiral Nelson following the battle of Trafalgar in 1805.

Further north of Rosia Bay, in the Napier Battery, you will find the most imposing of all the cannons kept in the enclave. It is called the **100-Ton Gun**, from 1870. It could send projectiles of almost a ton, and its shooting rhythm was of one shot every four minutes. It needed the as-

The 100-Ton Gun.

Ibrahim al-Ibrahim Mosque.

sistance of up to 35 men from different ranks. An interpretative centre next to the cannon gives you all the details about this powerful weapon.
Between Rosia Bay and Camp Bay Beach you will find the most important battery of the enclave: **Parson's Lodge**. Since 1956 this place ceased to be under military custody and is now being used for military training.
Before you reach Punta Europa, where the lighthouse stands, there are two temples of interest: the **Ibrahim al-Ibrahim Mosque,** a work of recent building and the **Shrine of Our Lady of Europa**, which is much older. Originally, this shrine was a mosque which, following the Spanish conquest in 1462 was consecrated as a catholic chapel. A simple wooden statue of the Virgin with the Child was placed on the altar and an oil lamp in its bell tower for the navigators crossing the Strait. Since then the chapel acquired fame and popularity and is a centre of pilgrimage. However, throughout its history, the temple and the image suffered several vicissitudes. In 1540 a raid of Turkish pirates plundered the temple and robbed all the valuable objects, and subsequently, a

wall was built around it, which no longer exists.
In 1704, following the British occupation, the navy again stripped the chapel of all its belongings and the statue of the Virgin was mutilated and thrown into the sea. But as they were made of wood, the pieces floated on the surface. A fisherman found them and gave them to Father Juan Romero de Figueroa, a monk who was in charge of the Cathedral and took them to a safe place in Algeciras. The chapel that had been abandoned as a place of cult, was seriously damaged during the Great Siege. Before then, since many Gibraltarians wanted to get it back, a replica of the statue was made that is still kept in the Cathedral. With the help of Pope Pío IX, Bishop Scandella brought the original statue back to Gibraltar in 1864, but as the chapel was being used as a military post, a provisional one was built in St. Bernard's Road.
Finally, in 1961 the old chapel was handed over by the militaries and the works of restoration started. The original statue of the Virgin was placed again on the altar and bishop Rapallo consecrated the chapel on October 5th 1980.

Punta Europa Lighthouse.

General view of the East slope of the Rock.

THE EAST SIDE OF GIBRALTAR

Abrupt cliffs that barely leave space for construction define the East coast of the Rock. You can reach it through the road along the edge of the Rock, part of which runs under a long tunnel. In all, the East coast reaches a length of a bit more than two kilometres and has three beaches: **Sandy Bay, Catalan Bay and Eastern Beach**. The most interesting is Catalan Bay, also known as La Caleta, with a nucleus that originated with Genoese settlers who dedicated themselves to repairing ships. At present, several pubs are concentrated there where you can have a meal or a snack. On one side, one of the most important hotels of Gibraltar stands, the Caleta Palace Hotel.

Between Sandy Bay and Catalan Bay, the slope of the Rock has been used to create a recurrent system for the recollection of rainwater. This is one more evidence of how the Gibraltarians take advantage of the few resources they have. Big galvanised steel sheets, nailed into the rock collect the water through different channels.

General view of Catalan Bay.

Sandy Bay and the water collectors.

The beach of Catalan Bay.

Catalan Bay from the terrace of Caleta Palace Hotel. ▷

INDEX

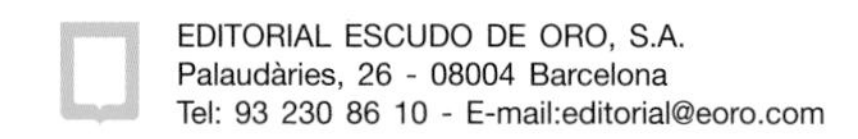

EDITORIAL ESCUDO DE ORO, S.A.
Palaudàries, 26 - 08004 Barcelona
Tel: 93 230 86 10 - E-mail:editorial@eoro.com

I.S,B.N. 84-378-2332-3
Printed by FISA - Escudo de Oro, S.A.
Legal Dep. B. 1493-2002